and

Simon Barrow

presence
and prophecy

a heart for mission in theological education
study guide

CHURCHES TOGETHER
IN BRITAIN AND IRELAND

CHURCH HOUSE
PUBLISHING

Church House Publishing
Church House
Great Smith Street
London SW1P 3NZ

Churches Together in Britain and Ireland
Inter-Church House
35–41 Lower Marsh
London SE1 7SA

ISBN 0 7151 5549 0

GS Misc 689

Typeset in 10/12pt Franklin Gothic

Printed by Halstan & Co. Ltd, Amersham, Bucks

Published 2002 for the Board of Mission of the
Archbishops' Council by Church House Publishing
and Churches Together in Britain and Ireland.

Tel: 020 7898 1557; Fax: 020 7898 1449;
copyright@c-of-e.org.uk.

contents

acknowledgements

This study guide has been produced on behalf of the Mission Theological
Advisory Group of the Archbishops' Council and of the Churches'
Commission on Mission of Churches Together in Britain and Ireland.
Thanks go to those individuals and groups who assisted in commenting
on the practicality of the material, to Sarah Roberts for expediting
production so effectively, to Lesley Butland for her efficient copy-editing,
and to the Laurelville Mennonite Church Centre, Mount Pleasant PA, USA,
and the Metzler/Roths for facilities to complete the final text. This study
material was compiled by Simon Barrow of Churches Together in Britain
and Ireland. But the whole MTAG process and the writing of the full report
and *Transparencies* is hugely indebted to Anne Richards, Mission Theology
Adviser to the Board of Mission of the Archbishops' Council, Church of
England. She advised on this material. Views expressed in this publication
are those of the author and do not necessarily reflect the opinions of MTAG.

chapter 1

welcome: setting the scene

Presence and Prophecy: a heart for mission in theological education (CHP/CTBI, 2002) is a report aimed at assisting all those involved in formal and informal education of adults, both lay and ordained, in the churches of Britain and Ireland. It has been produced by the Mission Theological Advisory Group (MTAG) – a joint venture of the Archbishops' Council's Board of Mission (Church of England) and other traditions (including Church of Scotland, Roman Catholic, Church in Wales, Methodist, Congregationalist) through the ecumenical Churches' Commission on Mission of Churches Together in Britain and Ireland.

The purpose of this Study Guide – which can also be used in conjunction with the CHP/CTBI book *Transparencies: pictures of mission through prayer and reflection* (2002) – is to make the report as usable, accessible and helpful as possible to a wide group of people.

Presence and Prophecy has to meet a number of needs. It is directed primarily towards those responsible for overseeing, managing, developing, supporting and setting the context for theological education within our churches. Its purpose is not prescriptive but exploratory. It seeks to promote a deepening conversation about how church-related learning can serve the mission of God in today's world. It is not MTAG's business to tell people how this should be done in detail – the range of possibilities in our churches is too wide, and the Group that produced the report recognizes its own particular commitments and limitations.

Even so, *Presence and Prophecy* has been written out of the deep conviction that empowering Christian education is vital to equipping the people of God for mission and its outworking in ministry. Mission perspectives should inform and shape all our teaching and learning – that is, both the style *and* content of what we do together.

If better, mission-focused theological education for the twenty-first century is to become a reality then a wide range of people will be involved in its reformation. So this Study Guide is consciously aimed at helping parish groups, ordinands, students, mission enablers, ecumenical groups and the broader Christian public get to grips with the issues. But its central concern is not 'churchy'. It starts from the challenges we face in everyday life and in a rapidly changing world. These are where we believe God is to be found – in the places of practical engagement from which mission in the biblical tradition proceeds.

chapter 2
how this study guide works

Presence and Prophecy is a big book covering a wide range of themes within its overall focus – how God's mission shapes and permeates church-related theological education. This Study Guide aims to make the report more manageable by breaking it down into smaller sections. Here is what is on offer.

overview and summary

On pages 4–5 you will find *an overview of the report written in twenty short points*. This will enable you to see in outline what it is saying and how its argument links together. The summary that follows (pages 6–11) is *a brief digest of what is in each chapter*. Rather more detail has been provided for chapters one and two, since this material on the world we live in and God's response to it is foundational in all that follows. The overview and summary will prepare you to 'skim' the whole report, to read it from beginning to end, or to focus on specific sections. We all approach things differently. These précis allow maximum flexibility and control. Of course you may find that *your* summary has different emphases!

sample study sessions

At the heart of this guide are *five study sessions* (pages 19–30) which cover part one of *Presence and Prophecy* (on the context for theological education in the world, God's response to the world and learning styles), plus selections from part two (the common curriculum components), and part three (future directions). Each of these sessions is recommended to last two hours. We have tried to combine activity, reflection and devotion in each. The more time you can spend the more you are likely to gain.

different study options, pointers and advice

We are aware that each group is different in its needs and capacities. The sample study sessions are aimed at providing a general study process. But they are only templates. On pages 12–13 you will find suggestions about *other study routes and possibilities*. There are indicators about how to handle the report with specialist concerns in mind (evangelism, students, etc.). Many using this material will already have much experience in leading groups, but there are some *tips and warnings* for all of us just in case!

further resources and ideas

These include suggestions on pages 31–2 for using *an accompanying volume of prayer, reflection and devotional material – Transparencies*, also available from CHP/CTBI. There are also indicators of wider implicit issues, key questions and general discussion ideas – 'bite sized' options, in other words. There is also a *Feedback* form and information about a follow-up *web site*. Let the debate continue …

chapter 3

what's in *Presence and Prophecy*?

a. overview: the core message in 20 short points

Here is a brief précis of the overall approach and argument of *Presence and Prophecy*. This summary draws upon, and provides a context for, each section of the book. The first twelve points are adapted from the Preface and Introduction, especially. The remaining eight are expanded further in 'Key Concerns and Findings' in this Study Guide (pp. 6–11).

1. *Presence and Prophecy* looks at how a changing church in a changing world needs to re-equip itself for effective ministry and mission in the twenty-first century. (Preface: Why we did it, pp. v–viii.)

2. It shows how the Church, the whole people of God, is caught up in a lifelong journey of learning.

3. 'Theological education', in all its many forms and varieties, is the way in which people are equipped and resourced for discipleship.

4. Sometimes existing church-based education actually *deskills* people. The aim of this report is to show how it can *empower* us as we travel and learn together.

5. Our starting point is Jesus Christ crucified and risen. He is our pattern for mission, for witness and service in everyday life.

6. God's love, embodied in Christ, overflows into the world. It is revealed in history and can be perceived within the radical shifts of contemporary culture.

7. Christians are called, therefore, to respond to God's initiative with bold experimentation rooted in tradition. We call this approach 'mission as jazz'. (Introduction, pp. ix–xi, and pp. 175–6.)

8. The missionary task in Britain and Ireland today has two key dimensions: presence and prophecy.

9. A conscious Christian *presence* within our culture must be nurtured and developed. That also requires *prophecy*, discerning the nature and effect of God's upside-down kingdom.

10. At the heart of this twofold mission lies God's constant, transformative concern for the whole world.

11. God's love in Christ calls his followers to particular words and deeds that demonstrate what this love offers and requires in specific situations.

12. It also calls for a wider 'missiological perspective' – the capacity to see how everything we say and do as Christians may assist (or block) God's redeeming purposes.

13. This is our framework for re-examining the theological formation of all Christians, lay and ordained, in today's church.

14. *Presence and Prophecy* starts by giving an analysis of the modern world and a picture of God's relationship with it as the context for ministry and mission. (Part 1: 'Settings', pp. 3–43.)

15. The report then looks critically at what is being taught, both formally and informally, within the churches. It examines how mission perspectives can be brought to bear in studies such as Church history, Bible, worship, pastoral care, and doctrine, as well as seeing how these also raise challenges for contemporary mission studies.

16. The emphasis is on a transforming perspective for core elements of fixed curricula in traditional theological education. (Part 2: 'Illuminations', pp. 75–188.)

17. The report says that all education and learning in the church now needs to make the changing nature of the world – and God's purposes for that world – the central concern from which all else flows. (Part 2, continued in Part 3: 'Heartenings', pp. 191–211.)

18. The disengaged nature of much theological education, and the abstract way it is offered, act as barriers to growth for many people.

19. Therefore *Presence and Prophecy* emphasizes participatory styles of teaching and learning, the breadth of the world context, and linking theory with practice (pp. 44–71).

20. There is a concluding bibliography for further reading, pointers to other resources and an index of key topics and references (pp. 226–42).

b. summary: key concerns and findings

part 1: settings

chapter 1: the world we live in

Britain today, along with much of the 'developed' world is characterized by:

- individualization: the increasing emphasis on the importance of self over community in different spheres of life (pp. 3–5);
- 'having the best' rather than 'getting better': an increasing emphasis on quality of life as represented by material possessions (pp. 5–6);
- rootlessness: a feeling of dislocation, and a tendency to lack direction or clear identity (p. 6);
- retreat from engagement: 'spiritual' life is seen as a shelter from risky endeavour and from the pressures of a changing world (pp. 6–7);
- globalization: the complex network of political, financial, cultural and ecological forces that shape us in ways that often seem beyond our control (pp. 7–12);
- communications: the bombardment of information, the dominance of IT in the lives of many people (pp. 9–10).

So we need to rethink:

- money and *God's* 'investment' in us: the relationship between how we are valued and how things get valued (or priced) in our world (pp. 10–12);
- jubilee: the biblical tradition of periodic release from the burdens of wealth and poverty, and the restoration of fairness (pp. 12–14);
- ethics: examining the consequences of our actions, looking at what and who really count, developing a liberating sense of relationship and duty towards each other, the creation and God (pp. 14–15).

how people live

We are increasingly shaped by:

- networks: communities of interest and concern, not just geographical communities (pp. 15–16);
- science and technology: our increasing reliance on know-how and equipment beyond our immediate control (pp. 16–17);
- perfection: our inflated image of how things 'ought' to be (pp. 17–18).

what people think

We also have to contend with:

- plurality: our changing attitude to living with a wide range of people of other religions and life-stances (pp. 19–20);
- spirituality: the search for wholeness and contentment, for a sense of life as a rewarding journey (pp. 19–20);
- Christ and life outside the church: the diversity of belief, Christ in the world, the spirituality of those who don't go to church (pp. 20–22);
- cynicism about religious institutions: the growing gap between experience, belief and religious belonging (pp. 22–3);
- story: God's story as our story? How do the different 'stories' of our lives link? (p. 23);
- holy places: recovering a sense of sacredness in particular locations and in ways of being (p. 24).

chapter 2: the world as God sees it

According to our developing understanding of the biblical story and tradition God relates to the world:

- from the heart: mission is the overflow of God's love into and for the world, seen in the experience of the Trinity (pp. 25–6);
- through constancy: God's continual and persistent presence and effect is to be found among us (pp. 26–7);
- in Jesus' mission: God's purpose is in bringing about a new order, the kingdom, through his (Jesus') life, death and resurrection (p. 27);
- by 'ministry' and through 'mission': different ways and emphases in describing the activity of Christians in response to God (pp. 27–9).

chapter 3: the 'marks' of mission

Unpacks the five major elements of modern Christian mission as the call:

- to proclaim the Good News (gospel) of the kingdom (pp. 30–31);
- to teach, baptize and nurture new believers (p. 31);
- to respond to human need by loving service (pp. 31–2);
- to seek to transform the unjust structures of society (p. 32);
- to strive to safeguard the integrity of creation and to renew the earth (p. 33).

A list of seven practical responses is offered (pp. 33–4).

chapter 4: people in ministry and mission

Understanding theological education as a function of the whole Church: helping us to put faith into practice through the vocation of work, through ministry in the community, and through forms of ordained ministry oriented towards supporting mission engagement (pp. 35–7).

chapter 5: some stories

Practical examples of ministry and mission in the neighbourhood and the wider world, including the role of prayer, dealing with power, the value of worship, and the use of church-related buildings (pp. 38–43).

chapter 6: styles of teaching and learning

An exploration of how we learn in different ways, and how God can be seen in the biblical tradition to model active learning and not just abstract 'knowing'. Engagement and encounter is central. Jesus' teaching was based on a responsive attention to people and relationships. Openness, questioning, exploration, growing awareness, discernment, tutoring and mentoring are all involved. Christian learning is about a widening sense of vocation before God, in the company of others (the Church) and for the sake of the world. Our teaching methods and places of learning need to be like this: to draw upon the depth of tradition and the courage of experimentation. Education is about transformation and involves learning to use power responsibly. The focus should be on equipping all, not just a clerical minority, and upon what can be learned from the great variety of God's world (pp. 44–71).

part 2: illuminations

chapter 7: mission as presence

How does the actual content of theological education help to support Christian presence and prophetic witness? Core theological questions are identified concerning God, Christ and the world (pp. 75–7).

chapter 8: mission and Church history

Suggests that an idea of 'where we are coming from' is vital to a sense of mission, but that we must not tell history out of manipulative self-interest. The key question is 'what difference does it make?' for the transformation of the world and of people's lives. A missionary understanding of history proceeds from a God who acts towards us in love and works towards a fulfilled future. Worship is the place where this sacred story is dramatized. We need to learn how to hear untold parts of the story, to pay attention to difference, and to uncover distortions of the past that may harm our present and future (pp. 78–97).

chapter 9: mission and the Bible

The biblical story of God's active love in the world is overlaid with competing narratives and perspectives. Responsible mission requires that we hear these different voices and attend to core scriptural concerns: Who is God? What is the divine will and how does it work? How should we respond to God? The biblical drama is one we participate in and live out. As we do so, key questions arise about the specific claims of the Christian story in relation to God's universal purposes, about patterns of partnership between the human and the divine, about blessing and judgement, ethics and election, power and servanthood, the Church and the nations. The historical claims about Jesus Christ arising from the New Testament and their difficult relation to the claims of the Hebrew Scriptures are especially important to us for rethinking cross-cultural mission. Biblical specialists should help us attend to these matters (pp. 98–132).

chapter 10: mission and worship

In the churches there are often divisions between those who give priority to right worship and those who stress right action. In the New Testament, 'service' is one: worship and daily living are apiece, and mission is what takes place in daily life as we respond faithfully to God. Worship is a transformation in the meeting between God and humanity. Praise refigures the world. It celebrates saving events. It also meets a human need in us to respond to real worth and value. Liturgy provides a pattern for seeing the world and acting in it. It narrates the coming together of God's story and ours. In the light of this, we need to pay attention to the content and performance of words, music and images. The sacraments are both expository (they show things) and performative (they achieve things). Hymns and prayers shape our language and communication. Repentance, forgiveness, sharing and sacrifice are central to worship and mission. Intercession calls God's future into being. Yet worship is also a place of Christian divisions and exclusiveness. How do we handle these in a missionary way? (pp. 133–51.)

chapter 11: mission and pastoral care

If mission is love overflowing from the heart of God, pastoral care of people-in-community is one of its key expressions. Caring also involves a degree of missionary confrontation with the sources of wounding and injustice in our world. It brings fresh awareness of self and others, linking what we learn of the world through worship, engagement, psychology and spiritual direction.

The tensions between directive and non-directive approaches to care are important for both presence and prophecy. The chapter concludes with sharp observations about the language and meaning of mission from pastoral practitioners, sometimes indicating how mission has been used for abusive as well as for saving purposes. Mission has much to learn here, as well as much to contribute (pp. 152–73).

chapter 12: mission and doctrine

Missiology has sometimes claimed to be the mother of theology: Doctrine is a response to missionary questions about the identity of God, Christ, the Spirit and the world. But the Western world has historically controlled this discourse of theology and in many ways continues to do so. If doctrine is about ways of coherently understanding the breaking open of the world by the Word, then it needs to be open to truth and insight from six continents and not just one or two. Much attention also needs to be paid to other faiths and to different religious cultures: African and pre-Christian ones, for example. Mission asks questions about the location and purpose of the theologian. In responding to the four 'publics' for theology – the society, the Church, the academy and other faith communities – it becomes possible to move from the theology of mission to proper missionary theology. Doctrine is also a matter of church tradition, human self-knowledge and 'structures for understanding'. In moving across experience, understanding, judgement and decision, we are taken to the threshold of action. Exploration, doctrine and mission therefore belong to one movement (pp. 174–88).

part 3: heartenings

chapter 13: mission as prophecy

The last section of the report outlines some answers to the question 'What would theology be like with mission at its heart or centre?' (p. 186.) The concern throughout has been for mission perspectives that permeate other disciplines within the educative ministry of the Church. But there is also a role for mission as a separate subject – a place where the missionary heart can be nurtured and disturbed. Out of dialogue with, and learning from, other disciplines some major (shared) challenges emerge: the theology of God's action in the world, conversion, creation and eschatology, relations with people of other faith, practical evangelism, and the missionary nature of hope. In all this it becomes important to ask about the 'end' of mission, about the work of the Holy Spirit among differing 'spirits', about the moral responsibility of specific missionary enterprises, about the role of proclamation in truth-seeking, about how faith is shared appropriately among people of different cultures and religions, and about dealing with failure and frustration wisely. In the long view we may see ourselves modestly but committedly as 'prophets of a future not our own' (Oscar Romero from Michael J. Walsh, *Archbishop Oscar Romero: The Voice of the Voiceless*, Orbis Books, 1995) (pp. 191–211).

chapter 14: conclusion

Presence and Prophecy does not end with a neat 'package' of solutions to 'problems' in theological education within the churches. It does not set out to promote a simple cause but to stimulate a deeper and better informed conversation among those with responsibility for Christian formation at all levels. The key proposal is that a developing Trinitarian account of God's overflowing love in and for the world ought to be at the heart of teaching and learning; that mission perspective and focus helps us to make sense of trying to walk in God's ways. The report argues that transformation (involving our intellects, emotions and spirits) should be at the core of all that is done in 'theological education', all within the context of a changing and demanding world (pp. 212–13).

chapter 4

how to use *Presence and Prophecy*

a. plotting different study route options

The five sample study sessions (pp. 19–30) offer the opportunity to
overview the whole report, with options to select material along the
way. This is the 'pre-digested' approach. There is a linear logic to the
organization of the text, but it is also desirable to plot your own 'journey'
and to vary the depth and intensity of your study. Indeed, you may find it
more rewarding to do that. Having a leader (or a leadership group) invest
time in familiarizing themselves with the text and adapting it to the needs
of the church/group is likely to produce the best results.

first principles

Presence and Prophecy begins with a picture of fast-changing Western
society, provides a missiological 'reading' ('what is God up to in all this?'),
and then looks at styles of teaching and learning adapted to different
needs. It goes on to examine specific elements of theological education
(Bible, Church history, worship, pastoral care, doctrine) from the
perspective of mission. It concludes with suggestions about how a
missionary understanding of the world and of the task of theology can
help reshape what we teach and how we learn in our churches.

four primary 'ways in' to the report

1. *The 'contextual' approach.* It is possible to start with an exploration of
   the human setting that shapes us. You might take key indicators from
   chapter one and ask members of your groups to devise presentations
   on each – with specific examples and stories that illustrate the
   challenges and opportunities you face in your setting. (Material from
   study Session One, pp. 19–20 will assist with this). You can then ask
   what possible missionary responses are open to you. The group might
   devise some options, with pros and cons, before responding to the
   ideas in chapters 2, 7 and 13. Chapters 4 and 5 provide examples

from different settings. On this basis, you can begin to devise your own 'learning curriculum' and to ask how best to make use of existing resources and educational facilities provided by the churches and allied institutions.

2. *The 'tradition-centred' approach.* A different method would be to begin with *what the Bible and the churches have understood* about the nature and task of mission. Critical resources can be found in chapters 2, 3, 9 and 11. You can devise a chart of different approaches – ranking them both in terms of what your own church teaches and what you actually practise. The challenges and opportunities of your context (chapters 1, 5 and 11) can then be reviewed in relation to what you have discovered about the vocation of the Church. Now list the priorities (in terms of content and style) for the kind of theological education that will best equip you.

3. *The 'ecclesial' approach.* Alternatively, you might commence with *the worshipping and serving community* (chapters 11 and 12), asking: Who are we? Who and what do we belong to? What is our calling? Who do you think God wants us to be? (p. 30.) A next step would be to consider what, in the culture and society you are part of, weakens or strengthens your identity and vocation, and how God's story in Jesus Christ enables you to respond. Where are your opportunities for learning and for equipping people on this journey and how are they organized?

4. *The 'learning centred' approach.* Finally, your departure point might be to look at *what is actually taught in your church or institution*, how it is conveyed, how it is received and why it is organized in the way it is (chapters 4 and 8 to 12 *passim*). Questions about the shape of mission (chapters 2, 3, 7 and 13) will be relevant to assessing the adequacy of existing programmes/options, and their ability both to convey the riches of the tradition and to address the changing world (chapters 1 and 5).

In each case you will be choosing a route that:

- makes sense to the people in your group and their way of doing/ seeing things;
- opens up new challenges and vistas, whatever your starting point;
- chooses prime examples or passages from the report for critical reflection;
- incorporates the experience and expertise of people in the group;
- leads from a picture of where you are to a picture of where you might go next, by way of some practical and theological analysis.

b. pointers for particular audiences

Both the pre-formatted study sessions and the routing options above
presuppose a 'generalist' group, while leaving open more specialist options.
A different approach would be to focus on some very specific issues or
styles of learning.

1. *Parish and local church groups* may be interested in looking at how
   they learn as part of their Christian vocation – but may also find the
   analytical and schematic approach of the report challenging. A range
   of short stories and examples is therefore included in the text, especially
   in chapters 1 (pp. 4–5, 8–9, 17–18, 22–4) and 5 (pp. 38–43). These
   can be used to explore (for instance) the relationship between particular
   patterns of mission and the changing world. Direct experiences of
   theological education (Chapter 6, pp. 50–54, 58–60, 63–4, 68–9)
   are also relevant here.

2. *Mission enablers* will be interested in the relationship between the
   'marks' of mission (Chapter 3) and what is taught formally within the
   churches (chapters 8 to 12). How does this assist or detract from
   specific mission tasks (the 'seven possibilities', pp. 33–4) or from
   the need for presence (Chapter 7) and prophecy (Chapter 13)?

3. For those involved in *pastoral work and concerns*, the question of how
   'mission' and 'ministry' fit together (Chapter 4) and how they make
   sense of each other will be particularly relevant. The creative tension
   between the two, not least in relation to the way they are taught,
   comes out in Chapter 11. It informs the dual approach of presence
   and prophecy (chapters 2, 3, 7 and 13).

4. *Bible study circles* may wish to start with Chapter 9 on mission in the
   Hebrew Scriptures and the New Testament. Chapter 8 on Church history
   also contains foundational material (pp. 81ff.). What is the biblical basis
   for the 'marks' of mission (Chapter 3) and how are biblical traditions –
   plural – taken up within doctrine (Chapter 12) as an elaboration of the
   nature of the missionary God (Chapter 2)? The section on teaching and
   learning (Chapter 6) also contains key ideas about the pedagogy of God
   in Christ (pp. 46–9).

5. *Adult educators* will obviously be interested in Chapter 6, concerning the
   missionary interpretation of core elements of the traditional curriculum
   (*passim*), and in the question about how mission perspectives impact
   the ongoing debate between didactic and experiential modes of
   teaching and learning. The question of whether training for particular

kinds of ministry deepens or divides the sense of the *laos*, the whole people of God, within the 'sent' body of Christ runs throughout the report. See particularly pages 36, 41–2, 84–5, 212–13.

6. Those working as *evangelists* will note that there is no single section on 'evangelism'. This is not because a form of mission is being advocated that downplays witnessing or disciple making. On the contrary, it is so much at the heart of the encounter between God, culture and faith that it runs *throughout* the report. There is specific focus on evangelism in its historic forms (Chapter 8, pp. 157–73), in the Scriptures (especially pp. 104f), and as an expression of mission as prophecy (pp. 169–70, 205–8). To what extent and how do Christian presence and Christian action get expressed verbally and in proclamatory form (pp. 204–8)?

7. For those who are *inter-faith practitioners*, the challenge of missionary encounter and dialogue as a medium for authentic witness is intrinsic. This report takes up the prophetic urgency of interreligious issues (pp. 198–200, 202–4), recognizes their doctrinal significance (pp. 187–8), and tackles their role in theology (pp. 181–5). A number of stories and examples assume an interfaith background, and the issue of pluralism is tackled in chapters 1 and 2.

8. Finally, those with an interest in *liturgy and worship formation* (Chapter 10 and also pp. 7, 28–9 and 61), *systematic theology* (chapters 2, 3 and 12) and *history* (Chapter 8 and pp. 6, 117, 137–8, 199–200 and 211) will find their concerns thoroughly implicated in the analysis of *Presence and Prophecy*. *Students and ordinands* may want to use the report to review what they are being taught and how they are learning. (See also point 4 on page 13.)

c. for group leaders: opportunities and constraints

Though it is advocating a more active, participatory and mission-focused approach to theological education, *Presence and Prophecy* is a report aimed primarily at church leaders and those with specific interests in mission and learning. Because it is advocating mission permeation of all aspects of our curricula and pedagogy, its remit is wide. It therefore has to condense a good deal of analysis. This means it is not a 'beginners'' text. People with little formal education or background in the issues raised will struggle with the 'raw' book. That is why we have tried to break down the material (above) and to include story content so that what is said is thoroughly based in everyday human experience. The accompanying book *Transparencies* (CHP/CTBI, 2002) also features a more visual approach.

The key recommendation is 'don't bite off more than you can chew'. In addition, remember these points:

- *Be aware of the wider picture*. Even if you are tackling a small section of the report, it is helpful to have a couple of people present who have read all of it.

- *Be clear about your aim(s)*. For instance, are you wanting to reflect further on the overall shape of mission; on specific mission-focused ministries and how they are equipped; on the relationship between theology and the context for mission; on learning and teaching styles; or on some combination of these? (Make sure you know why you are studying what you are studying).

- *Be clear about your objective(s)*. For example, is it to widen your perspective, to relate mission to another major area of concern, to look at the possibility of making specific changes to learning programmes, to assist a review of lay/ministerial/ordination/missionary curricula? (Specify your expectations and goals at the outset. Are you mostly *exploring*, *explaining* or *deciding*?)

- *Be honest about your intentions*. Is your focus on the report a lens for your current concerns, or your concerns a lens for reading the report? Or a bit of both? How will you know the difference?

- *Be realistic about your group*. Divide the total time available by the total number in the group. Deduct 'presentation' or reading time. This will help you to work out how much genuine scope there is for participation. Better to do less in greater depth and leave people wanting more than to attempt the unachievable.

- *Be aware of people's learning styles*. Some are happy to listen/read and tackle questions. Some prefer an activity or discussion starter. Some want to read in advance (and some don't or won't). Some are stimulated by story or visual material. Almost all need to know why they are here, what they will do, and how they will know if they have achieved something.

- *Adapt your methods* to meet your aims, objectives and the nature of the group. (This is why this Study Guide tends towards options rather than prescription.)

- *Make adequate time for preparation*. Ideally, the leader should spend as much time preparing as the group spends meeting. A highly skilled facilitator can read an excerpt or relate an argument, get people talking in pairs, bring them together in plenary and draw out conclusions, an action list and referrals for further study. But it rarely happens as easily as that. Work out and time how you will do it, bit by bit.

- *Do not over-elaborate*. Allow plenty of space for discussion and for the unexpected issue. Do not be anxious that people will dry up. Make space at the end for 'drawing together' your deliberations and considering next steps.

- *Think 'appropriate scale'*. With a small group of six to eight you can go into a lot of detail and try a number of paths informally. With a large group of fifteen or more you need more structure, less material, and a clear process/leader for deciding which route to take if new options present themselves.

- *Take responsibility*. Use the ideas in this Study Guide, but don't assume someone else knows your needs better than you do. Do it your way. If it doesn't work, try something a bit different next time.

- *Challenge committee culture*. Church bureaucracies can kill study processes by imposing their usual, stiff, formal style on something that is (by its nature) more exploratory and challenging. Don't let them. Do it differently. Model your practice on your message and vice versa. Mission means movement.

chapter 5

study sessions: templates for exploration

leaders' notes

- *Overview.* These units have been designed as adaptable templates for the creation of study sessions to explore the overall content of *Presence and Prophecy*. Each is timed at two hours. We recommend an additional ten-minute break in the middle. Session One and half of Session Two look at Part 1 of the report ('Settings'). The second half of Two and Sessions Three and Four concern Part 2 ('Illuminations'). The short third section ('Heartenings') is addressed as part of Session Five.

- *Style.* We have included in each session an activity, reading and discussion, prayer, a time for 'recommendations' and visual/song elements. You may want to add a Bible reading at the end. These elements will suit people of different personalities and learning styles. *You are free to lengthen or omit different sections.* These sessions assume a group of eight to fifteen people.

- *Length.* You should reckon to spend at least 10 minutes on 'welcoming' and the opening prayer; 40 minutes on the activity (25 for doing, 15 for reacting); 50 minutes on reading, reflecting and gathering (in smaller groups and as a 'plenary'); 15 minutes noting recommendations, and 5 minutes – longer if you choose – in concluding prayer.

- *Aims.* Each session intends:

  (a) to help people understand and respond to a section of *Presence and Prophecy*;
  (b) to relate what is in the report to people's own experience and perception;
  (c) to draw conclusions for further study or action;
  (d) to operate in a climate of openness and prayer.

- *Background.* If possible, add on further time at the beginning of the first session to look at the structure, content and argument of the report as a whole. (Starting with a half-day and a meal would be ideal for these purposes.) Section 3 of this Study Guide could be photocopied and issued in advance, along with the Contents (p. iii) and Conclusion (pp. 212–13) from *Presence and Prophecy*. Reproducing these as OHP acetates or a wall-chart would give people a visual sense of 'where we are and where we are going'. It is best to avoid comment at this stage to allow space for the members of the group to interrogate and interpret the material as they go through it.

- *Preparation.* Ask everyone in the group to have read chapters 3 to 5 (pp. 30–43) before the first session. These will get them thinking about the meaning of mission.

- *Before each session.* Allocate the sections of the report to be read and studied privately. It will be difficult to come to the material 'cold'. Suggest people use a pencil to put *a tick* by points they agree with, *a cross* by things they disagree with, *a question mark* by things they are not sure about, and *an exclamation mark* by thoughts that strike them as new or provocative.

- *Welcoming.* An 'ice breaker' is suggested for the beginning of the first session. The time for this (about ten minutes) can be reallocated to reading/reflection or closing devotion in subsequent sessions. The questions considered in the opening icebreaker also recur as part of the conclusion of Session Five.

- *Recording, etc.* Encourage members of the group to take their own notes. You will also want to appoint a 'recorder' for each session, someone to handle any equipment needed (flipchart, OHP) and someone to be 'housekeeper' (tea, windows, heating etc.).

session one: changes – living and learning

Remit: Chapter 1 ('The world we live in', pp. 3–24), Chapter 6 ('Styles of teaching and learning', pp. 44–71). It would be possible to split this session into two, one on the context of mission and the other on learning about mission – in which case the activity could bifurcate into a community survey and a congregational/student organizational survey. Supplementary material: Transparencies, chapters 7 ('Absence') and 9 ('Desire').

1. prayer

Use the following prayer with illustrative slides or display pictures/images:

> By giving, re-living
> By stilling, refreshing
> By drowning, immersing
> By raising, re-versing
> You, Lord, deliver us.

(Graham Kings, *Transparencies*, p. 41.)

2. welcoming

Invite members of the group to introduce themselves, to say what interests them about these sessions and to specify what they hope to get out of them. Remind them of the three chapters they have read (see *Preparation* above) and of the précis of the report at the beginning of this Study Guide.

Collect on a wall-chart a collage of words or phrases that summarize what people feel is the core of Christian mission. Ask: how many of these reflect (or react against) what is said in these chapters? Note that this is our starting point, but do not discuss in detail. This is simply a barometer of the group's starting point. *Bring the chart to subsequent sessions so that you are aware of it as a background. Reconsider it in detail at the end of Session Five.*

3. reading, gathering, exchanging

Divide the group into two and allocate them space to talk in. Give each group an extract from, respectively, chapters 1 and 6 of the report. (The summaries on pp. 6ff. of this Study Guide will help – especially with choosing from Chapter 1, which is long.) In each case ask:

- How does this reflect our own experience?
- Where does our experience vary from what is described?
- In what way has the setting for mission (Chapter 1)/challenge of learning about mission (Chapter 6) changed in our lifetime? And for whom?
- To what extent (theologically) does the way the world is 'set the agenda'?
- How is 'learning' related to the nature and purposes of God?

Allow at least 15 minutes to compare what you are saying. (This exercise can be extended by another half hour or so if you are starting with a half-day session.) Note key areas of concern for your context. Note also areas of agreement and disagreement within the group. How might these be handled in terms of the church's mission, and in terms of *how* you learn and teach? What new and significant insights strike you?

4. activity

On the basis of your explorations, work together (initially in pairs or threes) to devise a street survey for use in a local community. Start together by noting the key features of the area, using the insights from chapter one to help you. Then think of the different 'learning styles' that might be reflected in the questions (e.g. some practical, some observational, some reflective, some to do with 'the big picture'). The focus of the survey should be 'what is most important in my/our life?' The aim is to help the Church discover how people see life and (implicitly) faith.

You will need to decide whether, how and why it is/is not desirable to include 'religious' questions; and how much to focus on individuals v. 'community infrastructure'. Compile a large list of questions, then edit them to ten and then five. What takes priority and why? Note your own learning as a group from this exercise. How could it usefully be developed? *(Note that survey development usually depends heavily on testing and refining questions with the intended interviewees, so that we discover what questions help those who answer them as well as those who ask them.)*

5. recommendations

How can what you have learned together be carried forward for the purposes of mission/teaching in your context? List five key action points or recommendations (which can include further study). To whom are these addressed and who will carry them forward?

6. closing devotions

Choose a song and a prayer familiar to your church/group.

session two: possibilities – God's presence

Remit: *Chapter 2 ('The world as God sees it', pp. 25–9), Chapter 3 ('The marks of mission', pp. 30–34), Chapter 5 ('Mission as presence', pp. 75–7), Chapter 14 ('Conclusion', pp. 212–13). Supplementary material:* Transparencies, *chapters 4 ('Hope') and 8 ('Loss').*

1. prayer

Use the following prayer with illustrative slides or display pictures/images:

> Creator God,
> you have painted the whole creation in its richness;
> you see us as we truly are.
> Help us to see beyond our broken world
> and know the truth and beauty you reveal to us.
> Amen.

(Transparencies, p. 19.)

2. activity

Before the session select three local, national and international papers or news magazines. Split the group into three and allocate one to each. Ask them to rewrite a story as if it were a Scripture. How is God present, by what means, to what ends? It would be helpful to get people to do this on OHP acetates so that the results can be shared easily. Come together as a group. What are the similarities and differences in our approaches to this task and its outcomes? What are the resources at our disposal for discerning God's presence to and engagement with the world in which we live? What do we learn from this exercise? To what extent is it (and is it not) possible to develop a 'God's eye view' of the world? What do we learn about our understanding of God? How does this enable us to reflect more on 'God as learner' (think back to Chapter 6 and what you may have said about this in the previous session).

3. reading, gathering exchanging

As a whole group, remind yourselves of the marks of mission (Chapter 3). Which ones echo most strongly for you? Where do you see your primary participation? (You may want to recall the preparatory reading from chapters 4 and 5 – people in ministry and mission, plus some illustrative stories.) Share two or three selected readings from chapters 2, 5 and the Marion Mort quotation from the conclusion (p. 212). Discuss. Then spend time responding to the questions in Chapter 7 (pp. 75–6):

- Who is God?
- How should we respond to God?
- Who are we?
- How should we live before God?
- What must we do?

You could divide the group at this point so that half is considering the questions:

- Who is Jesus Christ for us today?
- What does it mean to follow Christ?
- What does it mean to make Christ known?

It may be helpful to consider these as blocks of interrelated questions, rather than to tackle them one by one. Compare your answers. How does our starting point (God and the world, Christ and discipleship) lead to different emphases? How are the two sets of questions related for a Christian? Most importantly: how does what you are saying about God and Jesus Christ relate to what you said about the setting of mission and human learning in the previous session? Where are the consonances, tensions and gaps? How can these be addressed effectively within the church as a (theological) learning community?

4. recommendations

(as Session One)

5. closing devotions

(as Session One)

session three: traditions – history and Bible

Remit: *Chapter 8 ('Mission and Church history', pp. 78–97), Chapter 9 ('Mission and the Bible' – a. Hebrew Scriptures, b. New Testament, pp. 98–132). Supplementary material:* Transparencies, *chapters 5 ('Cross') and 6 ('Bible').*

1. prayer

Use the following prayer with illustrative slides or display pictures/images:

> Turning the world upside down
> is the charge against Silas and Paul;
> Turning its values the right way up
> is the Kingdom's promise and call.
>
> (Graham Kings, *Transparencies*, p. 34.)

2. activity

The following role play about the transmission of Good News properly
requires four groups plus leader: that is, a minimum of nine in the group.
It would be possible with three groups, that is six plus leader.

Each group is given a 'scroll' (an A4 sheet of thin white card), plus a pen
and elastic band. They are given ten minutes to write down the Good News
of God's dealings with their community. (This can be based on actual
experiences of the church in their context.) The scribe must also do his/her
best to remember what is written. Then the scroll is 'sealed' with the band.

When each group is ready, the scribe is sent to the next group. The scribe
reports verbally the group's Good News. The recipient group remembers
what it can and nominates a messenger to go to the next group to relay
the message – and so on, until each group has heard a remembered
version of each of the written scrolls. (No notes may be taken by anyone
during this process.)

At the end, the groups come together to report the Good News they have
heard to each other. The *furthest* verbally transmitted version of each
(the version heard by the last group to receive it) is announced. Then the
original scroll is unfurled, read and compared with that final verbal report.

As a group: what has changed in transmission? What has been cut?
What has been simplified? What has been added? What has been
elaborated – and why? (The aim of this enjoyable exercise is to gain
some first-hand experience of how earliest tradition was handed on
and the factors involved.)

3. reading, gathering, exchanging

The material on Church history (Chapter 8) and on the Hebrew and
Christian testaments (in Chapter 9) is very full. According to choice, you
should focus *either* on the biblical material and have someone summarize
key points from the chapter on history, *or* combine readings from Chapter
8 and one section of Chapter 9. Again, working in two groups and then
coming back as a whole to report and discuss will be a way to maximize
the time available. Use and adapt the questions at the end of these two
chapters (pp. 97, 116, 132). The blocks of adapted questions might be
as follows:

- How does an appreciation of the historical context help us to understand the wider issues impacting Christians in mission in particular settings?
- What difference does our understanding of both the 'mistakes' and 'good faith' of our forebears make to the task of mission today?
- How can we discern 'good fruit' from distortions in our past?
- How does the study of history give us responsibility for the future of the Church?

And on the biblical tradition, generically:

- How and why did the biblical accounts we have come to us in the shape they are today?
- Do we love the Bible enough to dance with it?

On the Hebrew Scriptures:

- How does study of the Hebrew Scriptures help us to know what God is like?
- What does it mean to be a 'holy' people in today's world?
- What are we to make of 'election' and the apparent violence of God in some texts?

Or on the Christian Scriptures:

- What were the central intentions of Jesus and the reasons for his death?
- How and why did the early Church get started in the way it did?
- What might the Gentiles have expected Jesus to say and do?
- In what way are the New Testament documents missionary in intent or design, and what does this mean for us today?

End by talking about how history and the biblical record are taught and transmitted today. What is our part and responsibility in this?

4. recommendation

(as Session One)

5. closing devotions

(as Session One)

session four: transformations – pastoral care and worship

Remit: *Chapter 10 ('Mission and worship', pp. 133–151), Chapter 11 ('Mission and pastoral care', pp. 152–172). Supplementary material: Transparencies, chapters 3 ('Praise') and 10 ('Transformation').*

1. prayer

Use the following prayer with illustrative slides or display pictures/images:

> Unchanging God
> you see this world we have made for ourselves,
> full of wealth, poverty, luxury and want.
> Teach us to see beyond the seductions of desire
> and to find our satisfaction in your love.
> Amen.
>
> *(Transparencies, p. 48.)*

2. activity

Give each member of the group two sheets of A4 paper taped together horizontally. Each person draws a line across the centre and marks on that line five-year periods (beginning with their date of birth) to create a 'time line'. They are then invited to mark on that time line significant points of both 'transformation' and 'transfiguration' in their lives – times of change and of spiritual growth or illumination.

Together discuss: What role do the Christian community, family, friends, neighbours and other carers have on our lives? Where do growth, development and celebration happen? What is the role of worship and pastoral care in nurturing us towards witness and service? You might consider (with additional time) creating a communal 'time line' around the room. How are worship and pastoral activity involved in preserving what is good and changing what is detrimental in our lives?

3. reading, gathering, exchanging

Now turn to chapters 10 and 11. Select readings from each for small group and/or large group discussion, as before. On worship you may find the following italicized quotations helpful (Lordship, p. 133; praise and thanksgiving, pp. 135–6; confirmation, p. 137; hymnody, p. 141, holiness, pp. 143f. worship and conduct, p. 146; liturgy, celebration and participation, pp. 147–8; hope, p. 149; and mystery, p. 150). Questions that might be used or adapted (p. 151) include:

- How is the relationship between 'the saving acts of God', the contemporary setting and the worship of God effectively related in our churches?
- What understanding of God, the world and humanity is being promoted by the form and content of our worship?
- What is the relationship between worship and work ('service') both in theory and in practice?
- In what way is worship/liturgy a foundation for and component of mission?

On care, compare the answers you would give to the questionnaire (see major headings from p. 157 through to the end of the chapter) sent out to pastoral practitioners. The stories contained throughout the chapter bring the issues highlighted to life and can form a further basis for reflection. See also the quotations concerning pastoral care theory (pages 152–5). The following questions (cf. p. 173) may be useful:

- What is the relationship between mission and pastoral care?
- Is the primary purpose of pastoral care to bring people into, or relate them to, the Church?
- Where would you ensure appropriate boundaries between mission and pastoral ministry?
- Are 'mission' and 'maintenance' really competing activities?

4. recommendations

(as Session One)

5. closing devotions

(as Session One)

session five: directions – theology and prophecy

Remit: Chapter 12 ('Mission and doctrine', pp. 174–88), Chapter 13 ('Mission as prophecy', pp. 191–211). Supplementary material: Transparencies, chapters 7 ('Vision') and 2 ('Sacrifice').

1. prayer

Use the following prayer with illustrative slides or display pictures/images:

> Our Father
> you are for turning;
> turning us round
>> upside down
>> inside out.
> Help us to give ourselves
> to your revolution of challenge and love,
> through him who called for
> turning and trust
> Jesus Christ our Lord,
> Amen.

(Graham Kings, *Transparencies*, p. 57.)

2. activity

Read through Oscar Romero's prayer/poem ('Prophets of a future not our own') on page 210. What does this tell us about doctrine (how we formulate what we believe) and prophecy (the impact of faith on how we live)? In the light of your response, divide into three groups. Ask each to take the prayer of Jesus – the 'Lord's Prayer' or 'Our Father' and re-express it for, respectively, three different audiences: one per group.

Address your prayer so that it can be understood by those of another faith tradition, by a social action/community group (not primarily Christian), and by a group of scientists or other 'specialists'. The idea is to maintain the message of the prayer while using amplifications or dynamic equivalents to communicate what it is saying to those who may be unfamiliar with the basic concepts and language. (See, for example, how Graham Kings has adapted the Lord's Prayer in the opening devotion.)

What does this exercise teach us about the faith that has been handed down to us and about its transmission today? What practical issues and questions does it raise about the relationship between 'doctrine' and 'prophecy'?

3. reading, gathering, exchanging

Here you will need to break into two groups before coming back together to compare reflections and impressions. The first should read some extracts from Chapter 12. The question of 'whose theology?' and the dominance of Western models is clearly important (pp. 174–6). This extends into a discussion of academic vis-à-vis vernacular theologies (pp. 176–9), 'models' of contextual theology (pp. 180–184), and the four structures of understanding (pp. 185f.)
The last section asks:

● What would theology be like with mission at its centre or its heart?

It is suggested that you take this as the central issue of your time of reflection. See the six key points on pages 187–8 and the supplementary questions on page 188, which might be adapted as follows:

● How does the variety of theology help us to engage better in missionary conversation?
● How are Western theological models and assumptions rightly challenged in our changing world?
● How is our understanding and experience of God stretched through a mission perspective on theology?

Chapter 13 is concerned both with the prophetic dimension of mission (its capacity to provoke us into seeing the radical demands of God's transforming presence) and with the issue about whether and how mission should be a defined subject within a theological curriculum – as distinct from the ground and implication of everything else that is taught.
On the first question, see the story on page 193 as a starting point, and also the issue of conversion (pp. 194–5). There are also sections on the motivation and 'end' of mission (pp. 195–6f.), the work of the Holy Spirit (pp. 197–9), and evangelization in relation to received notions of mission (pp. 199–201).

This leads naturally into subject areas where there is an explicit missionary concern that cannot easily be subsumed: faith-meeting-faith (pp. 202–3), faith sharing (p. 202), evangelism (pp. 204f.), proclamation (pp. 205f.), sharing and accompanying (pp. 206f.), hospitality and embassy (p. 207), and the practicality of mission and evangelism (pp. 207f.). The chapter concludes with a reflection (pp. 209f.) on wisdom and hope. The questions on page 211 focus some of these concerns. You can either take an overview or focus on something specific that connects with your context/concerns.

4. recommendations

As this is the final session, you might want to extend this section. First, revisit the answers you gave to the initial questions you explored under 'welcoming' in Session One.

- How and why have people's viewpoints shifted?
- How has understanding developed?
- Where has prior experience been challenged?
- In what way has God been speaking through your shared explorations – both in agreement and disagreement?

Then collect your final list of recommendations for further action and study, with indications as to how these can be carried forward and by whom.

5. closing devotions

Conclude with Oscar Romero's prayer/poem 'Prophets of a future not our own', on page 210.

chapter 6

Transparencies: mission focus in practice

In addition to the report *Presence and Prophecy: a heart for mission in theological education* (CHP/CTBI, 2002), a separate but related volume called *Transparencies* (CHP/CTBI, 2002) has been produced. This book is designed specifically for use in parish groups, lay training, ministerial formation and other church educational settings. It puts the core message of the report into practice by offering *an engaged, critical, devotional model for theological reflection on daily life.*

- Each chapter – organized as a prayer and meditation session – takes 'mission' concerns as foundational. The language is not that of the narrow specialist, but of the Christian motivated *to re-understand the world through God's self-disclosure in Jesus Christ*. Out of God's overflowing heart come *new ways of acting and seeing*.

- *Transparencies* contains ten topics. Six arise directly from contemporary culture. 'Vision' is developed out of Douglas Coupland's famous Gen X story, *Girlfriend in a Coma* (with its inspiration in the music of The Smiths). 'Sacrifice' visits J. K. Rowling's famous *Harry Potter* books. 'Absence' reflects on the R. S. Thomas poem, *The Moon in Lleyn*. 'Loss' is the theme from Barbara Kingsolver's novel, *The Poisonwood Bible*. 'Desire' emerges from a visit to the Bluewater shopping centre. And 'Transformation' proves to be the surprising consequence of best-selling family TV movie *The Muppets Christmas Carol* (Columbia Pictures/Jim Henson Pictures, 1992, directed by Brian Henson).

- In each case we explore *the theological implications of 'secular' culture*. There are also four sections on explicitly religious themes: the hymns of Isaac Watts ('Praise'), Sister Wendy Beckett on *The Gaze of Love* ('Hope'), Jonathan Clarke's dramatic sculpture *Christ on the Cross*, and the Bible ('Evil', Judges 19–21).

- The idea is that the initial image or literary theme becomes a 'transparency' through which light passes as we pray, reflect and talk. The *convergence of transparencies builds up a fresh image* that poses questions to us about *what our lives might look like* in the service of mission. Each chapter contains prayers (some of them are used in the five study sessions here, pp. 19–30), excerpts and pictures, a meditation, discussion points, guidelines and resources.

- The material in *Transparencies* can be used both by individuals and groups. It is ideal for building up a process of theological and mission reflection with a lay group. All chapters can also serve as *a practical introduction to themes explored* in the report *Presence and Prophecy*: the use of the Bible, engagement with culture, history, spirituality, witness, the consumer society, and so on. Sample suggestions are made on pages 12–14 in this Study Guide.

lenses for reading: commentary on wider topics

Since the central contention of *Presence and Prophecy* is that the encounter of the faithful community with human society is the space where the gospel takes shape and the place from where theology must be done, a variety of wider topics is implicated in its treatment of theological education. Not all of these are identifiable by specific section or chapter. A number are implicit in our methodology rather than explicit in the content of our argument. Here are some key themes that deserve particular attention. We invite you to use the index, bibliographies and section headings in the report to explore them further.

the world church as a key resource for Christian learning

The Mission Theological Advisory Group is accustomed to 'thinking globally and acting locally'. The index and bibliography of the report indicate that Christian theology from Asia, Africa and the Americas has been formative in our thinking. The dominance of Western modes of thought has long been questioned in contextual theology. Most church agencies operate models of partnership founded on the recognition that mission is now 'from everywhere to everywhere' (Michael Nazir-Ali, *From Everywhere to Everywhere: a World View of Christian Mission*), rather than 'from the West to the rest'. Indeed, in the last 100 years Christianity has shifted its locus towards the South. It is polycentric rather than monocentric. Sociologist Grace Davie now speaks of 'the European exception' when describing the demise of religion in public life here.

Presence and Prophecy does not explicitly address the many arguments about the nature of world Christianity, secularization and desecularization (see MTAG's *The Search for Faith and the Witness of the Church*, Chapter 1), but it is rooted in an understanding that can no longer take 'our' version of events in Britain and Ireland as defining for 'Christian mission' *per se*. In many respects, cross-cultural mission prefigured other forms of globalization and can act as a critical ferment within current developments. Local churches in Britain need a much greater consciousness of their global identity as well as their local one. These issues are vital for re-founding effective theological education today.

This report is nevertheless concerned with theology and formation in our context (that is, taking proper responsibility for what is ours). We do not expect others – especially those with fewer resources – to do our work for us. But our work can only be done effectively by taking seriously the voices, experience and criticisms of Christians in other parts of the world. This is a dialogue of mutuality in which we speak for ourselves, but in consciousness of the Other and of the history between us. Increasingly interfaith perspectives are challenging the intra-Christian nature of our conversations just as global Christian voices are impacting our intra-cultural ones. Many of the new alliances (and new arguments) cross existing denominational and agency lines. The Spirit continues to blow afresh and theological education has to orient us to the kind of discernment this requires of us.

ecumenism and theological education

The existence and work of MTAG in its present form is part of the growing ecumenical destiny of mission theology in Britain and Ireland. The Group's work originated in the Church of England and has evolved to embrace a wider range of Christian communions through partnership with the Churches' Commission on Mission of Churches Together in Britain and Ireland. In a small working group not every tradition can be present. But all of us are conscious of the way that our thinking and outlook have been 'formed ecumenically' and of the responsibility this places upon us.

The flow of God's love has enabled us to perceive the riches in our different traditions and to seek a unity in Christ based relationally on 'gifts differing' rather than institutionally on homogeneous structures. We do not always agree, but it is trust and openness to the Spirit that have enabled us to produce a report together. From time to time there will be comments and references that betray a particular denominational origin. These should be seen as waymarks rather than obstacles.

Theological education is organized and practised in remarkably different ways in our different Churches. It is neither possible nor desirable to comment on each of these in detail. How the issues and opportunities depicted in *Presence and Prophecy* are taken up is a matter of ecumenical reception. So the work in this report is offered to all the Churches as part of an ongoing conversation about formation and mission. This is one model of being 'churches together' agreed at Swanwick in 1990 – initiatives from one section of the Christian community being offered to others for appropriation in ways that suit (and sometimes challenge) their needs and perceptions.

from 'laity' and 'clergy' to 'the whole people of God'

For some people the term 'theological education' implies, quite specifically, the training of ordained ministers and priests. MTAG has made it clear that we are adopting a much broader definition – indeed one that goes further even than the segmentations implied by 'lay training', 'clergy training' and all the other compartmental labels our Churches are apt to use. This is because the question at stake in *Presence and Prophecy* is about how we work together, across our different forms of organization, to equip the whole people of God for the purposes of God's mission in the whole world.

Particular specialisms, charisms and patterns of ministry are needed for this task. All are called, but not all in the same way. Important issues of ecclesiology arise as the Church in its diverse forms is shaped for mission. Again, *Presence and Prophecy* is not prescriptive in this area, but it does contend that the vocation of mission and the nature of the world in which mission is discharged are central to working out how to be church today.

chapter 8

discussion ideas

How different groups handle *Presence and Prophecy* will depend upon the culture and expectations of the people involved and the time available. For some, the need will be to find a way to break into the (inevitably) formal style of the some of the material. For others, it will be the formality of the *group* or committee that needs challenging! How often have you been in a discussion circle only to reach the most lively debate near the end? Here are three direct ways of breaking down inhibitions, getting to the group's core concerns sooner rather than later, and making connections with people's life experience.

1. following the story

There are a number of short stories and examples scattered throughout the report. These can be used as discussion starters in their own right. For example, if you are examining 'The world we live in' (Chapter 1) you will find ten illustrations: the conflict over choosing a church for a wedding (pp. 4–5); women's economic experience in Bangladesh and East London (p. 8); globalization in the video market (p. 9); church involvement in community regeneration (p. 14); 'network' living (pp. 15–16); ethics and stealing (p. 17); implicit religion (p. 18); the search for faith (p. 22); art and spirituality (p. 23); and religious buildings in a secular culture (p. 24).

These examples can be used as a way into the analysis of the chapter. You could ask people to act out – or create on paper in a small 'buzz' group – some dialogue associated with several of these incidents. Or you could collect experiences from the group that are similar or contrasting, as the basis for a wider conversation. You could also compare the experiences of theological students (Chapter 6) or of people in ministry and mission (chapters 4 and 5) with the experiences of those beyond or on the margins of the church as a way into discerning the particular issues for mission in your setting.

2. making life connections

The chapters in Part 2 ('Illuminations') contain less narrative material and they are comparatively dense in terms of content, but the issues they highlight can be fruitfully matched up with the imaginative pictures and literary illustrations from *Transparencies*. Both contrast and consonance are possible. Indeed *Transparencies* emerged from the prayer and reflection times that preceded the detailed discussions at each meeting of the Mission Theological Advisory Group. There was often no planned connection, but we discovered surprising convergences between our meditations on culture and our deliberations about theological education in the light of mission.

For instance, the chapter on the story from Judges opens up issues that are explored in Chapter 9 of *Presence and Prophecy* on teaching the Hebrew Scriptures. Obvious connections also exist between Jonathan Clarke's sculpture of the Cross (and less immediately obviously between the 'transformation' in *The Muppets Christmas Carol*) and issues of mission in the New Testament. 'Desire' (the Bluewater shopping centre) raises profound questions for 'mission as presence' (Chapter 7 of the report). Similarly, the loss experienced in the novel *The Poisonwood Bible* has significant implications for the way we teach Church history (Chapter 8), and the vision emerging from Douglas Coupland's *Girlfriend in a Coma* has odd resonance with the architecture of worship. Many other linkages are possible.

3. opening up issues through questions

Many chapters in *Presence and Prophecy* include discussion questions at the end. Some of these depend upon studying the text that precedes them. Others could equally serve as preliminary explorations to set the scene for a reading and group discussion. The section on mission and the teaching of doctrine, for example, would be usefully introduced by first getting the group to respond to three initial questions adapted from those on page 188:

- What sort of theology do we find in (and beyond) written, academic studies?
- In what ways do people ordinarily encounter Christian doctrine? How do we hear *their* theological discourse? What difference does this make?
- How do people of other faiths help us to think more deeply about *our* theology?

Equally, group leaders may find it more useful to read the section of the report they are about to study and devise their own questions to introduce it to a particular audience. For missionaries or mission partners examining chapter nine (New Testament), these might include:

- To what extent (and why) do you see the New Testament documents as products of mission?
- In what ways can scriptural texts be *mis*used in mission contexts?

- What are the arguments for and against New Testament studies being kept *separate* from mission studies?

The aim here is not to reach conclusions but to compare the instinctive response of the group to the ideas developed by MTAG. At the end of the session the questions can be revisited to see how people's understanding and opinion has shifted.

chapter 9
what next?

web site

The Mission Theological Advisory Group is an ongoing ecumenical project. The last MTAG report, *Search for Faith and the Witness of the Church* (Church House Publishing, 1996) examined patterns of belief outside formal religious institutions and how the Churches might respond creatively, though not uncritically, to 'where people are'.

Presence and Prophecy looks at how Christian people are equipped for the task of both inculturation and witness in this context. The next phase of work (2002–c.2005) will explore the task of 'apologetics' in a plural, postmodern setting – how we best give an account of the grounds and shape of the hope within us.

You are invited to be part of this work. Along with the 2002 report, this Study Guide and *Transparencies*, we will be launching a modest web site in November 2002. Its address will be:

www.geocities.com/missiontheologygroup/

You can also access it through: www.ccom.org.uk, click on MTAG icon. Additional resources are available in the 'downloads' section.

The site, which will develop over time, will include feedback and discussion areas, additional resources and links. We will be happy to receive submissions from those reading and responding to *Presence and Prophecy*. The Feedback form overleaf will also be on the site, but if you prefer you can photocopy it and send it to:

Dr Anne Richards, Mission Theology Adviser, Church House, Great Smith Street, London SW1P 3NZ.

feedback

We would appreciate your comments on the *Presence and Prophecy* report. What you say will influence the future direction and style of MTAG's work.

1. What is your overall assessment of the quality of the report? (please mark an 'X' at the appropriate place along the line)

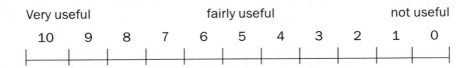

Very useful   fairly useful   not useful

10   9   8   7   6   5   4   3   2   1   0

2. What aspect of the report did you find most helpful and why?

3. What aspect of the report did you find least useful? How could it have been improved?

4. What is your assessment of the presentation and organization of the report?

5. Any other comments or suggestions?

bibliography

Atkinson, David, *God So Loved the World: Towards a Missionary Theology*, SPCK, 1999.

Barrow, Simon, and Smith, Graeme (eds), *Christian Mission in Western Society*, Churches Together in Britain and Ireland, 2001.

Board of Education, *Tomorrow is Another Country: Education in a Post-modern World*, Church House Publishing, 1996.

Craig, Yvonne, *Learning for Life*, Mowbray, 1994.

Hinton, Jeanne, *Changing Churches: Building Bridges in Local Mission*, Churches Together in Britain and Ireland, 2002.

Hope, Anne, and Timmel, Sally, *Training for Transformation* vols 1–4, ITDG Publishing, 1999.

Hull, John, *What Prevents Christian Adults from Learning?*, SCM Press, 1985.

Merriam, Sharon, and Caffarella, Rosemary, *Learning in Adulthood: A Comprehensive Guide*, Jossey-Bass, San Francisco, CA, USA, 1999.

MTAG, *Presence and Prophecy: A Heart for Mission in Theological Education*, Church House Publishing/Churches Together in Britain and Ireland, 2002.

MTAG, *Search for Faith and the Witness of the Church*, Church House Publishing, 1996.

MTAG, *Transparencies: Pictures of Mission Through Prayer and Reflection*, Church House Publishing/Churches Together in Britain and Ireland, 2002.

Nazir-Ali, Michael, *From Everywhere to Everywhere: A World View of Christian Mission*, Collins, 1991.

Oxley, Simon, *Creative Ecumenical Education: Learning from One Another*, World Council of Churches, 2002.

Vogel, Linda, and Knox, Alan, *Teaching and Learning in Communities of Faith*, Jossey-Bass, 1999.

related titles from the Mission Theological Advisory Group

Presence and Prophecy

A heart for mission in theological education

This thoughtful and stimulating report asks what kind of teaching and learning experiences can help Christians to become people with hearts for mission. It takes a fresh look at elements of the theological curriculum and suggests a new vision and hope for all the Churches. *Presence and Prophecy* is ideal for anyone involved in theological education, whether in formal training for lay and ordained ministry or in other aspects of theological study.

£11.95   0 7151 5548 2

Transparencies

Pictures of mission through prayer and reflection

What do Sister Wendy, the Muppets, Harry Potter and a sculpture of Jesus on the cross have in common? The answer is that they can all provide a focus for prayer and reflection on mission which in turn can be used to help us see more clearly how God is at work in and through our contemporary culture.

This imaginative collection of prayers and reflections, road tested by the ecumenical Mission Theological Advisory Group, is suitable for all kinds of prayer and study groups and can be adapted to a Lent or Advent course.

'Shows that prayer is the heart of our witness.'
David Atkinson, Bishop of Thetford

'Helps us to think afresh about God's mission.'
David Kerr, Belfast Central Mission, Northern Ireland

£6.95   0 7151 5550 4